MW01154322

Yvonne Krishnan

PREDATOR

PLANTS

20 QUESTIONS KIDS ASK ABOUT CARNIVOROUS PLANTS

Contents

Introduction 1

How do I know whether a plant is a carnivorous plant? 2

How many types of carnivorous plants are there in the world? 3

Should we be afraid of carnivorous plants? 4

What are the biggest carnivorous plants? 7

Why have some carnivorous plants become extinct? 9

How are carnivorous plants different from other plants? 11

What sort of environments do carnivorous plants thrive in? 13

How do carnivorous plants capture their prey? 15

Does the carnivorous plant have a digestive system? How does it work? 18

How do carnivorous plants avoid eating the insects that pollinate them? 20

What happens if a carnivorous plant digests a poisonous insect? 22

What is the life cycle of carnivorous plants? 24

Why do carnivorous plants have periods of dormancy? 26

What kinds of acid do carnivorous plants produce? Are they dangerous? 28

What animals live inside carnivorous plants? 30

How do Venus flytraps move? Do they have muscles? 32

Venus flytraps sound really cool. How can I grow one? 34

What can I feed my Venus flytrap? 36

How often should I feed my Venus flytrap? How long does it take for a Venus flytrap to digest what it has trapped? 38

Do Venus flytraps have flowers? 40

Activity Sheets 42

Glossary 50

Solutions to Activity Sheets 51

Introduction

Welcome into the world of Carnivorous Plants where plants don't just have pretty flowers and leaves and are eaten by animals. Instead, in the world of Carnivorous Plants, the reverse happens and these plants become **predators** that trap their **prey** and digest them.

Predator Plants gives us an introduction into how such plants came to exist and looks at the environments in which they are able to **thrive**. This book explores 20 of the most common questions that we all want answered about these beautiful, interesting and weird plants.

ENTER THE WORLD OF *PREDATOR PLANTS!*

How do I know whether a plant is a carnivorous plant?

A Bromeliad
[CC BY 2.5 Photo by Abe Ezekowitz via Wikipedia Commons]

Carnivorous plants have a number of special features to attract, trap, kill, and digest prey, and absorb **nutrients**. Some plants may have one or two of these **characteristics** but not all of them. **Glands** that **secrete** sticky substances are found in many plants. Bromeliads like the one pictured above and a few other plants have pitcher-like tanks. However, according to some experts, a plant is carnivorous only if it has all three of the following characteristics:

1. It has developed in such a way that it is able to catch its prey
2. It is able to digest its prey in a way that can be absorbed by the plant
3. The plant has a way of absorbing the nutrients

2

How many types of carnivorous plants are there in the world?

There are more than 650 different species of carnivorous plants that attract, trap and digest their prey with the help of special structures that have evolved over millions of years.

It is important to know that carnivorous plants trap and digest their prey for nutrition because many plants trap insects for **pollination** purposes. For example, the Jack-in-the-pulpit in North America catches insects with its flowers and then releases them after pollination.

Jack-in-the-pulpit plant
[CC BY 2.5 Photo by Ivo Shandor via Wikipedia Commons]

The **genus** with over two hundred species is Utricularia, also known as bladderwort, a plant with tiny bladders (or utricles). Sadly, humans have caused many carnivorous plants to become extinct so if you do come across one in the wild, treat it with care. Take all the pictures you want. However, leave it alone because there are now very few of such plants' sites left that any careless action on our part will lead to us harming them.

Utricularia reniformis
[CC-BY-2.0 Photo by Flickr User Dick Culbert]

Fuzzy Pitcher Plant
[CC-BY-SA-2.0 Photo by Flickr User Beatrice Murch]

Should we be afraid of carnivorous plants?

After all they prey on all sorts of insects and have been known to consume frogs and rats. Why shouldn't we be afraid? What's to stop them from taking a huge bite out of our arm or leg if we get too near?

I saw a movie the other day about a mad scientist that turned carnivorous plants into man-eating creatures. Can this happen in real life?

The short answer to this question is "No". As long as we're all larger than insects, frogs and rats, we're safe from these plants' traps.

Even if we were to somehow come into contact with the digestive enzymes they produce, our flesh would not melt off our bones because these enzymes are weak and will have no impact on us.

Many people are fascinated by carnivorous plants. However, there are some who find them creepy because of the idea that plants are able to eat animals instead of the other way around. This feeling is encouraged by the movies that have portrayed monster sized Venus flytraps devouring humans with no apparent difficulty or terrorizing fleeing crowds of people.

Deadly or flesh eating plants have appeared in many movies. This list is just a small sample.
- The Ruins (2008)
- Batman & Robin (1997)
- Little Shop of Horrors (1986)
- Attack of the Killer Tomatoes (1978)
- Venus Flytrap (1970)
- Day of the Triffids (1963)

Reality is very different. These plants have no way of hurting us. In fact, it is often the other way around with such plants being more and more difficult to find growing in the wild because of us humans and increased pollution.

Cephalotus follicularis
Source: www.hantsflytrap.com

What are the biggest carnivorous plants?

The biggest plants are reported to be in Malaysia. They are the endangered Nepenthes rajah, which grow mainly on Mount Kinabalu and the neighboring Mount Tambuyukon in Eastern Malaysia. These plants grow in areas where the soil is loose and permanently moist.

The largest carnivorous plants are in the genera Nepenthes and Triphyophyllum with traps that have evolved to capture creatures as large as frogs and rats although they don't do that very often.

Large lower pitcher of *Nepenthes rajah*. Mount Kinabalu, Sabah, Borneo
[Public Domain Photo by NepGrower via the English Wikipedia Project]

The Nepenthes rajah have large pitchers which measure up to 40 cm long and 18 cm wide. Another interesting thing about this plant is its relationship with treeshrews, which some researchers believe may be why they have grown to be so large. Treeshrews often mark their feeding territory by defecating directly into the plants' cups providing the plants with nitrogen.

The Common Treeshrew
[CC BY 2.5 Photo by Stavenn via Wikipedia Commons]

What is a treeshrew?

It is a squirrel-shaped mammal with a body that measures between 6 and 9 inches and weighs approximately 6.7 ounces. It has sharp nails and a bare patch of skin above its long nose. It also has a distinctive pale band at the shoulder.

Why have some carnivorous plants become extinct?

There are two main reasons why this is happening. The first is because of what is happening in the environment i.e. pollution. Nitrogen is an essential nutrient for all plants. But carnivorous plants have evolved to live in environments that lack this nutrient by supplementing their diet with insects. However, industrial activities throughout the developed world have caused an increase in nitrogen pollution so that more of the element is seeping into soil via rainfall.

Round-leaved Sundew [CC-BY-SA-3.0 Photo by Michael Gasperi via Wikipedia Commons]

A study done on the round-leaf sundew plant found that plants in the southern bogs were getting more nitrogen from the soil instead of insects. You might think that this is not a problem because they are still getting the nitrogen they need but it is a problem for carnivorous plants. When the soil becomes nitrogen-rich, other plant species begin to "move in", leading to greater competition for needed resources. Carnivorous plants use more energy than non-carnivorous plants, since they have to operate and manage their complex system of traps to catch their prey. This makes them weaker competitors than other stronger, faster growing plants, and these other plant species could take over. By blocking sunlight or using all of the water in the ground, non-carnivorous plants can cause the population of carnivorous plants to decline, and even become extinct.

In addition to suffering from environmental changes like pollution, carnivorous plants are also suffering from their own popularity by poachers, who pinch plants like Venus flytraps to sell on the black market. Poaching has become such a problem that a new law was passed in December 2014 making it a felony punishable by 25 to 39 months in jail.

Venus Flytrap showing trigger hairs
[CC BY-SA 2.5 Photo by Noah Elhardt via Wikipedia Commons]

How are carnivorous plants different from other plants?

There is actually very little difference between carnivorous and non-carnivorous plants. Like all plants, carnivorous plants need nutrients to grow and flourish but the environments in which they are found have not always made normal plant processes possible so they have had to adapt to their environment and evolve.

Carnivorous plants stand out among all other plants because they are able to use their abilities that, when taken together, make the plant carnivorous.

Many different kinds of plants have insect-attracting structures such as colorful leaves and flower parts that produce sweet sugar secretions (like nectar). Others may trap and kill small animals using sticky hairs, thorns, cupped leaves, poisonous liquids, or a combination of these tactics. In some cases, it is known that the juices of dead animals can be absorbed through the surfaces of plant leaves.

Skunk Cabbage

For instance, tomato plants have "sticky" leaves and you may sometimes find dead bugs attached to them. The "skunk cabbage" produces fly attracting odors and frequently traps flies inside its flowers to ensure pollination. The Dischidia or ant plants have little pouch-like structures in which ants live. After a while, the plant sends roots into the pouch to absorb any ant remains and feces that have accumulated. This makes them similar to the carnivorous plants because they are getting part of their nourishment from the ants, but are they? Definitely not because the ant plant does not have all the three characteristics mentioned in the previous chapter, which are:

1. It has developed in such a way that it is able to catch its prey
2. It is able to digest its prey in a way that can be absorbed by the plant
3. The plant has a way of absorbing the nutrients

What sort of environments do carnivorous plants thrive in?

Carnivorous plants can be found in a number of different habitats that have some common environmental characteristics. These are mainly open areas with low nutrients that are moist or wet for at least part of the year. The most common habitat for these plants is in bogs and swamps, where levels of plant nutrients are low but water and sunshine are abundant.

A pitcher plant on a rock face in Palau

Botanists have discovered that carnivorous plants can survive without catching prey, but they believe that the extra nutrition they get from various prey helps the plants

13

grow faster and produce more seeds, allowing the plants to survive better and spread into new areas.

There are more than 650 different species of carnivorous plants found in the world with some growing in every continent except Antarctica. They are especially numerous in Australia, North America and South East Asia. Carnivorous plants do not like competition from other plants and tend to grow well in areas where other types of plants do not. In many cases they grow in places that have periodic fires which act to cut down on competition, keep their habitats open, and release nutrients into the soil.

For this reason, carnivorous plants do not grow well in areas where plenty of nutrients are available. This is because in these areas, the ability to capture insects is not considered an advantage and the plant would be wasting energy catching insects while other plants are putting energy into growing taller and stronger, leaving the carnivorous plant at a disadvantage.

How do carnivorous plants capture their prey?

Carnivorous plants capture their prey with traps, which are **modified** leaves. These leaves or traps may have either active or passive mechanisms.

Passive traps do not involve any movement on the part of the carnivorous plant. There are three types of passive traps. These are the adhesive, pitfall and the lobster pot. With the adhesive trap, insects are caught by the sticky substance secreted by stalked glands on the leaf surface. Sundews and butterworts have adhesive traps and insects are attracted to the leaves by what looks like nectar droplets and by the sweet smell of the secretions.

Heliamphora – The sun pitcher

With pitfall traps, animals are attracted to the trap by nectar and the flowerlike appearance of the traps. On the inside of the trap, there is a very slippery surface on which the prey lose their footing and slide down into the trap base. Sun pitchers and cobra lily are examples of plants with such traps.

The lobster pot is another passive trap. It is a one-way system trap in which prey can find their way in but cannot get out. Prey are encouraged to enter by the lure of nectar.

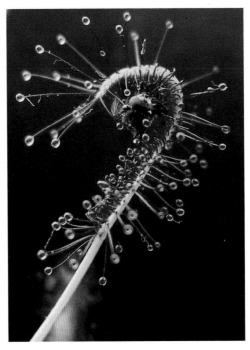

The leaf of a *Drosera capensis* "bending" in response to the trapping of an insect.
[CC BY-SA 2.5-2.0-1.0 Photo by Noah Elhardt via Wikipedia Commons]

Active traps are classified as such because there is movement involved in the trapping mechanism. These plants have sensitive trigger hairs and moving parts. There are three types of active traps. These are the curling flypaper, snap trap and suction trap. In the curling flypaper, the stalked glands actively bend toward the victim.

Some carnivorous plants have snap traps, which snap shut on the prey. Teeth like spines at leaf edges prevent the prey from escaping. This is the type of trap that can be found on Venus flytraps.

The last type of active trap is the bladder or suction trap, which can be found on bladderworts. As soon as a prey brushes against the entrance of the trap, the door instantly swings inward. The caved-in bladder walls then relax and pop open again creating a suction effect that flushes the victim into the trap interior.

Utricularia aurea
[CC BY 3.0 Czech Republic Photo by Michal Rubeš via Wikimedia Commons]

Does the carnivorous plant have a digestive system? How does it work?

When you eat or drink, whatever you consume goes in through your mouth and is mixed up with saliva, which breaks down the food a little before you swallow. Then it is pushed into the opening of your esophagus and moves down to your stomach. Your stomach stores the food you've eaten, breaks down the food into a liquid mixture and slowly empties the mixture into your small intestines. Food may spend as long as four hours in the small intestines so that nutrients from all the food you've eaten passes from the small intestines into your blood. Next stop for these nutrients: the liver! And the leftover waste - parts of the food that your body can't use - goes on to the large intestine. This stuff needs to be passed out of the body and comes out as poop.

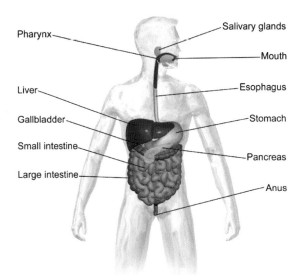

The Components of the Digestive System
Human Digestive System [CC BY 3.0 Photo by Blausen gallery 2014 via Wikimedia Commons]

Carnivorous plants are no different from humans in that, as soon as they have obtained their food, they have glands that secrete enzymes to dissolve proteins and other **compounds**. Other organisms may also be asked to help with digestion. The plants then absorb the nutrients that have been made available from their prey. For example, the Darlingtonia californica does not produce its own digestive enzymes and must rely on bacteria and commensals to digest its food for it.

Darlingtonia californica does not produce its own digestive enzymes.
[CC BY 2.5 Photo by Noah Elhardt via Wikipedia Commons]

How do carnivorous plants avoid eating the insects that pollinate them?

Carnivorous plants attract insects for two reasons – food and pollination - so how do they know not to consume the insects that pollinate them? According to experts, carnivorous plants have three mechanisms that help them separate prey from pollinator. The first is that their flowers are high above ground to attract flying pollinators while their traps are close to the ground to attract crawling insects. Secondly, their flowers bloom to attract pollinators first before their traps are developed to attract prey. Lastly, the flowers of the carnivorous plant rely on pollen or nectar to attract pollinators while their traps rely on scents and colors to attract their prey.

The Pitcher Plant and the Bee [Public Domain Photo by Flickr User Kaitlin Bellamy]

Does that mean that carnivorous plants never eat insects that have their pollen on them? Definitely not as accidents do sometimes happen and these plants will eat whatever falls in their traps. Just remember, eating pollinators is not in the plants' interest so they try to distinguish their flowers from their traps to attract the right kind of insects to each.

What happens if a carnivorous plant digests a poisonous insect?

Insects are usually poisonous to animals rather than plants so a carnivorous plant would probably be able to digest the insect like any other. However, the number of carnivorous plants that have become endangered as a result of habitat loss, poaching and pollution is increasing and scientists in the UK have discovered another threat to these endangered plants that might be contributing to faster and greater losses.

The culprit? Insects contaminated with certain metals like cadmium and copper. They can cause harm to these plants by interfering with the amounts of water and nutrients they are able to absorb.

Sarracenia leucophyllao
[CC BY-SA 3.0 Photo by Stephen C. Doonan via Wikipedia Commons]

Copper is an important nutrient for plant health and cadmium is a toxic metal found in a number of different products like fertilizers and metal coatings. Unfortunately, cadmium can accumulate in the environment because of improper waste disposal.

Tests were conducted to discover the effect of the two metals on plants with differing results. The plants were easily able to process and control the copper intake and faced no adverse effects.

By contrast, when house fly maggots contaminated by cadmium were fed to some endangered white-topped pitcher plants, it was found that the element accumulated in the plants' stems in way that was poisonous and could disrupt growth.

What is the life cycle of carnivorous plants?

Carnivorous plants are just like other flowering plants and have similar life cycles. **Step 1**: A seed will fall from the plant and, if conditions are right, **germinate**.

Step 2: The newly germinated seedling will put out roots into the soil. Because carnivorous plants are grown in soil with poor nutrition, it will produce specialized leaves to collect food. These leaves may be passive traps, such as the water-filled pitcher plant that drowns its victims; or active, such as the Venus flytrap, which snaps shut on its prey.

Darlingtonia Seedlings
[CC BY 2.0 Photo by Flickr User Incidencematrix]

Step 3: As the plant reaches maturity, it will flower, and be pollinated. The pollen will fertilize the reproductive part of the flower and seeds will form. For some plants this takes less than a year but for others, like the pitcher plant, it may take several years.

Eventually, the seeds will ripen and be disbursed to begin the process again. Sometimes, instead of flowering, the plant may also reproduce **vegetatively**. For example, Venus flytraps; often make little extra plants at the base of the main plant. These plantlets grow larger and continue the life cycle.

Why do carnivorous plants have periods of dormancy?

Some animals go into hibernation during winter because their main sources of food like insects or green plants are scarce. This deep sleep allows them to conserve energy and survive the winter with little or no food.

You might be surprised to know that some plants also experience a similar sort of state called dormancy. These include carnivorous plants that grow in habitats that are inhospitable during certain periods of the year. To survive these times, plants either produce seeds and die or they enter a dormant resting period.

1 year old Sarracenia seedling, waking up from dormancy
[CC BY-SA 2.0 Photo by Flickr User Aaron Carlson]

Some parts of the world do not experience much seasonal variation so carnivorous plants there may be grown all year round. Nepenthes, for example, which grow in the tropics, are grown all year round.

While some plants may be able to adapt to the tropics and allow you to get away with not providing a proper dormant period, the majority will eventually waste away after two years or so.

Different plants enter dormancy during different seasons. Many carnivorous plants rest during the cold season by forming dormant buds. Some sundews may stop growth and die back to the soil without forming any structure beyond a thick root system while other plants, such as Venus flytraps simply slow or stop growth.

Plants may enter dormancy not only because of the cold but because of excessive heat as well. Sundews of Western Australia are famous for their adaptations to the dry hot summers while Venus flytraps have a cool dormancy period of about three months. These plants desire chilly temperatures, but still expect some sunlight.

What kinds of acid do carnivorous plants produce? Are they dangerous?

Carnivorous plants do not produce any sort of acid. That is none of the corrosive kinds that will hurt you if you happen to come into contact with them. Instead, carnivorous plants produce digestive enzymes

The compounds that carnivorous plants make to digest food are quite mild. They are digestive enzymes like amylase and lipase which dissolve protein in their prey.

Using enzymes or the help of certain bacteria, carnivorous plants digest their prey through a process of chemical breakdown similar to digestion in animals. The end products are absorbed by the plants to enable their survival in poor environmental conditions. Most carnivorous plants are just like other green plants that make their own food by using the sun's energy to turn carbon dioxide and water into glucose (sugar) during photosynthesis. Existing in poor soil, carnivorous plants increase their nutrition levels by consuming any organisms that come near them.

The insect Pameridea, which only lives on Roridula (a South African carnivorous plant) eats other bugs trapped by the plant's sticky trichomes and then excretes nutrients that the plant needs.

[CC BY-SA-3.0 Photo by Denis Barthel Stueber via Wikipedia Commons]

Most carnivorous plants, such as Venus flytraps, sundews, butterworts, and many genera of pitcher plants all make their own digestive enzymes. Other carnivorous plants rely on bacteria to produce the appropriate enzymes. In this case, the plants themselves do not excrete the digestive juices. The food just **decomposes**, and the carnivorous plants absorb the **decaying** remains. Other carnivorous plants; rely on both their own enzymes and bacterially generated enzymes. This is called a symbiotic (or mutualist) relationship, because both organisms benefit from the **cooperation**.

What animals live inside carnivorous plants?

It may actually surprise you, but the traps of carnivorous plants attract many "guests" that coexist quite happily with carnivorous plants! This means that not all animals that come into contact with these plants end up as prey.

For example, insects that visit the flowers of these plants must be able to fulfil the role of pollinators without running the risk of ending up as the main course or dessert.

There is another group of animals that come into contact with carnivorous plants without any danger. These animals are called commensals. Commensalism is defined as "a relationship between individuals of two species in which one species obtains food or other benefits from the other without either harming or benefiting the latter." (Britannica.com) The term mutualism is also used in relation to commensalism. Mutualism is defined as an "association between organisms of two different species in which each benefits. Mutualistic arrangements are most likely to develop between organisms with widely different living requirements." (Britannica.com)

The Asian pitcher plants (Nepenthes) provide a habitat for a large number of animals and microorganisms. These include bacteria, fungi and unicellular animals that live in the pitchers. There have also been instances when some insects including ants have pulled captured prey out of the Nepenthes' pitchers, thus stealing from the poor carnivorous plant. But rather than trying to get rid of the ants, plants like the fanged pitcher plant actually house diving ant colonies, which suggests that the plants receive some benefit. What do you think this benefit might be?

A recent study found that fanged pitcher plants with diving ant colonies grow more quickly than those without the ants present. This led to the discovery that when the diving ants excreted their waste or died, the pitcher plants absorbed the nitrogen contained in the waste matter and ant remains.

The Australian rainbow plant provides a home to a bug that lives as a commensal on the plant and feeds on the prey caught on the plants glands. It is able to move freely on the surface of the plant without becoming stuck to the plant's secretions.

Nepenthes bicalacarata
[CC BY-2.0 Photo by Hans Breuer via Wikipedia Commons]

How do Venus flytraps move? Do they have muscles?

All plants have some power of movement, which can be divided into two types: nastic movements and tropic movements. Nastic movements are responses to stimuli but do not involve the growth of the plant. An example of nastic movement is the movement of the Mimosa Pudica or Touch-me-not plant.

Tropic movements or tropisms are directional movement of parts of a plant that occur in response to external stimuli such as light, force of gravity or chemicals.

But what about carnivorous plants? Some carnivorous plants can move extremely fast. They do not have any nerves or muscles so how do they do it? According to scientists, the Venus flytrap is capable of generating electronic signals. On the inside of each lobe of its trap are three or more sensitive hairs. As soon as anything touches one of these hairs more than once, the trap will snap shut.

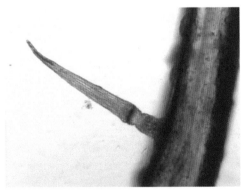

A close-up of a Venus flytrap trigger hair
[CC BY-SA 2.5 Photo by Martin Brunnert via Wikipedia Commons]

According to Alexander Volkov, a plant physiologist at Oakwood University in Alabama, the hairs are able to transform any touch into a small electrical charge that is transferred to the center of the trap causing it to snap shut faster than you would believe is possible. By closing in response to two closely spaced stimuli, the trap can avoid closing itself if something like a twig or leaf were to fall into it.

Venus flytraps sound really cool. How can I grow one?

According to the experts, the best way to grow a Venus flytrap is to copy their native habitat as closely as possible. This means that the soil, light and environment must be replicated so that it is similar to areas where Venus flytraps flourish. Let's look at the different elements that should be considered.

Growing a Venus flytrap – A checklist	
Soil	• Don't use regular potting soil. It doesn't provide the best drainage or water retention • Use a mix of sand and sphagnum peat moss • Soil should be nutrient poor, be able to absorb and hold plenty of water but be free draining
Light	• Carnivorous plants love the sun but avoid putting them in direct sunlight especially during the summer months • Note: Your plant is not getting enough sunlight if it doesn't have a pink interior or has long, spindly leaves
Humidity	• Environment must be humid
Water	• Use rain or distilled water to take care of your plant. Tap water is too alkaline and may contain too many minerals

Venus flytraps also have a yearly rest period called dormancy. This period begins at the end of summer and lasts several weeks to a couple of months. During this time, the flytraps' leaves will grow shorter and smaller and stay much closer to the ground. They still need light but less water so remember not to water so often that the soil remains wet for too long. This can encourage fungal and bacterial infections and rot.

So do you still want to grow or keep a Venus flytrap? I am sure that, like me, you are still tempted to. Just remember to do your homework so that you will be able to have a happy and healthy plant.

The Venus Flytrap [CC BY 2.0 Photo by Flickr User Mark Freeth]

What can I feed my Venus flytrap?

The Venus flytrap eats flies or other small insects. When you are feeding your plant, you have to ensure that the fly or bug you are feeding is alive. Dead insects are not suitable because the insect must move around inside the trap or the trap won't be able to consume and digest it. The prey moving inside the trap causes the trap to close and seal tightly before flooding the inside of the trap with enzymes that help digestion.

If you feed your plant a dead insect, even if the trap shuts, it will reopen soon after and you will find the dead insect lying there unconsumed.

What? But why won't my plant eat the nice, juicy bug that I've given it? Well, Venus flytraps are pretty savvy plants. They don't want to waste their energy trapping droplets of rain, small twigs or other stuff that fall into it by accident. So when the trigger hairs are touched just once, the trap closes very loosely. However, it there is a living bug trapped inside the plant, its continued movement would **stimulate** the trap to close more fully allowing digestion to take place.

What if you only have dead bugs?

If you only have dead bugs, first drop it into the trap so that the trap closes. Then gently insert a toothpick or a straightened paperclip through the gaps in the loosely closed trap. Wiggle the toothpick or paperclip, so the trigger hairs inside the lobes are stimulated. After a few minutes you will notice that the trap is settling into the next phase – digestion – which occurs when the trap stays closed for several days.

Venus flytrap [CC BY 2.0 Photo by Flickr User Blondinrikard Froberg]

Have a live bug but finding it a little difficult to feed it to your plant?
Cool the bug (don't freeze) for a few minutes, inside a jar placed inside a refrigerator for example, to cause the insect to become sluggish, easier to handle and less likely to escape from either your hands or the Venus flytrap.

Important note: Be sure to tell Mum what you're doing before placing the bug in the fridge!

How often should I feed my Venus flytrap? How long does it take for a Venus flytrap to digest what it has trapped?

The answer to this question depends on the individual plant. Once a trap captures a bug, it requires about a week to digest it. This means that if you have a large plant with seven or eight traps, one trap will reopen per day, ready for feeding.

However, you do not have to feed a trap right away just because it opens. Traps can go for weeks without being fed. They grow fine, just a little more slowly.

Welcome to hell [CC BY 2.0 Photo by Flickr User Mark Freeth]

When you're growing these plants from seeds and when the plant is small; you will see really small traps, which means that the insects these plants catch will also be small. Don't be tempted to fertilize your flytraps just because they're small. They don't need this because they receive nutrients from the insects they eat. During its growing period, a flytrap constantly produces new traps. Most traps last a month or two before turning black and falling off.

Outdoor plants will catch their own food but those grown indoors will require you to feed them and that's when the answer to the question, "What can I feed my Venus flytrap?" comes in.

Feeding tips

#1 Make sure the bugs you feed your Venus flytrap are no bigger than 1/3 of the trap. If the food is too big, the trap will not be able to create a proper seal, which will cause it to die or reopen without digesting its meal.

#2 Don't feed your Venus flytraps during dormancy. During this time, the plant is resting and saving its energy for the next growing season.

Do Venus flytraps have flowers?

Yes they do. Once a year in spring Venus flytraps produce a flower stalk (sometimes two or more) from the center of the plant. These usually grow from 8 inches to over 24 inches (20-60 centimeters) in height.

The idea of seeing a flower on your Venus flytrap might sound exciting but you might be surprised to know that many who have these plants don't allow them to flower because the flowering and seed-producing process uses up much of the stored food in the plants' **rhizome**. So it is usually recommended that the growing flower stalks be cut from weak or sick plants shortly after they appear. Only mature, healthy Venus flytraps should be allowed to flower and seed.

After pollination Venus flytrap flowers produce several dozen tiny, shiny black seeds. While most plants that bloom in the fall and produce seeds have adapted to wait until the cold weather of winter has ended before germinating, Venus flytrap seeds fall to the ground in the summer and usually germinate and begin to grow within 10 to 25 days.

Soft flowers of the deadly Venus flytrap

[CC BY 2.0 Photo by Flickr User Michael MK Khor]

Other carnivorous plants also have flowers. One example is the pitcher plant. Each flower is held on long stems that are well above the pitcher traps to avoid trapping potential pollinators. The flowers have an elaborate design which prevents self-pollination. The main pollinators are bees searching for nectar. This can be a difficult task for them because they have to push under the flap-like petals.

Activity Sheets

Crossword 1   43

Word Search   44

Words in a Word   45

Predator Plants Strike Again Double Puzzle   46

Crossword 2   48

Matching Terms & Concepts   49

Solutions   51

Crossword 1

Across

6. An essential nutrient for all plants
7. These help carnivorous plants digest their prey
8. This metal is harmful to carnivorous plants
9. Carnivorous plants use these to catch their prey
10. Carnivorous plants attract insects for ? and nutrition.

Down

1. This is a passive trap
2. Secrete sticky substances
3. Sweet sugary secretions produced by plants
4. A period of rest for carnivorous plants that is similar to hibernation for certain animals
5. Carnivorous plants grow on every continent except this one

Word Search

```
D  Y  F  F  A  T  S  I  C  D  Q  H  F  F  S
E  K  H  Q  Z  O  X  U  U  K  N  O  L  B  R
C  I  Q  M  W  G  L  I  X  U  Q  K  N  O  E
A  Z  I  E  O  I  E  G  T  C  Z  O  O  T  H
Y  A  K  O  T  Z  R  S  E  R  I  S  Z  A  C
T  H  Q  S  H  R  I  M  M  T  A  Y  N  N  T
N  C  M  C  M  T  E  N  A  I  K  P  M  I  I
X  E  N  V  I  R  O  N  M  E  N  T  S  S  P
M  K  F  O  Q  E  I  Q  E  J  Y  A  M  T  J
T  A  N  Z  V  L  D  W  V  I  A  R  T  S  C
R  O  O  I  L  Y  C  N  A  M  R  O  D  E  E
L  Q  R  O  P  S  D  O  I  N  J  H  D  J  S
F  H  P  R  X  E  S  X  Z  V  H  U  T  N  P
T  V  E  R  U  S  U  N  D  E  W  V  G  M  S
R  Y  L  C  I  Q  I  G  P  S  Q  A  M  Y  T
```

BOTANISTS   GERMINATES   PREY
DECAY   NUTRITION   SUNDEW
DORMANCY   PITCHERS   THRIVE
ENVIRONMENT   POLLINATION   TRAPS

Words in a Word

How many other words can you get from the word 'CARNIVOROUS'?
I have filled in the first blank. Try for 25 more words.

RACOONS	

Predator Plants Strike Again – Double Puzzle

EOPADRTR

PYER

SANVORCIRUO

TNSESIC

TTRSEINUN

SRHECPIT

NESDUSW

NASLDG

F

Unscramble each of the clue words. (Need some help, check out the next page)

Take the letters that appear in ◯ boxes and unscramble them for the final message.

Clues for Predator Plants Strike Again - Double Puzzle

1. Opposite of prey
2. Opposite of predator
3. The plants which obtain nutrients from insects
4. Most common source of nutrients for carnivorous plants
5. Carnivorous plants obtain this from insects
6. These plants have passive traps
7. Another carnivorous plant
8. Source of secretions

Crossword 2

Across

2. Traps last a month or two before turning this color and falling off.
7. The best way to grow a Venus flytrap is to _____ their native habitat as much as possible.
8. Color of the flowers of the Venus flytrap
9. Some carnivorous plants have passive traps and some have _____ traps.
10. These movements are responses to stimuli but do not involve the growth of the plant.

Down

1. A mammal that is attracted by nectar to huge Nepenthes rajah.
3. A group of animals that come into contact with carnivorous plants without any danger.
4. Some carnivorous plants rely on this to produce the appropriate enzymes to help with digestion.
5. This type of water is not suitable for carnivorous plants because it is too alkaline and may contain too many minerals.
6. These hairs can be found on the inside of each lobe of the Venus flytrap.

Matching Terms & Concepts

Write the letter of the correct term in the blank next to each sentence.

_____ Carnivorous plants with passive traps   a. Cadmium

_____ Carnivorous plants attract what with pollen and
          nectar.   b. Trigger

_____ When growing Venus flytraps, you must consider
          soil, light, water and _____.   c. Pollinators

_____ The name of a South African carnivorous plant.   d. Pitcher plants

_____ Carnivorous plant grown in the tropics.   e. Glands

_____ Period of rest experienced by some plants including
          carnivorous plants.   f. Active

_____ These secrete enzymes to dissolve proteins and
          other compounds.   g. Roridula

_____ Carnivorous plants have _____ and passive
          traps.   h. Humidity

_____ An element that is dangerous to Carnivorous plants. i. Nepenthes

_____ Sensitive _____ hairs enable the lobes
          of a Venus flytrap to snap shut when touched
          more than once.   j. Dormancy

Glossary

Anther	The pollen-bearing part of the upper end of the stamen of a flower
Botanists	A scientist who studies plants
Characteristics	Features or qualities belong to a person, place or thing that serves to identify them
Compounds	Made of two or more parts or ingredients
Cooperation	Working together for a particular purpose
Decaying	To cause something to become gradually damaged, worse or less
Decomposes	To decay
Environmental	Relating to or arising from a plant's surroundings
Genus	A group of closely related plants or animals (plural: genera)
Germinates	To cause a seed to start growing
Glands	Organs of the body or of a plant which produce liquid chemicals that have various purposes
Modified	To change something
Nutrients	Any substance which plants or animals need in order to live or grow
Pollination	The transfer of pollen from the anther to the **stigma**
Predator	An animal that hunts, kills and eats other animals
Prey	An animal that is hunted and killed for food by another
Rhizome	A horizontal underground stem capable of producing the shoot and root systems of a new plant
Secrete	To produce and release a liquid
Stigma	The part of the pistil (female part of the flower) where pollen germinates
Stimulate	To encourage something to grow, develop or become active
Thrive	To grow or develop successfully
Vegetative	A form of reproduction in plants by which new plants grow from parts of the parent plant.

Predator Plants Crossword 1

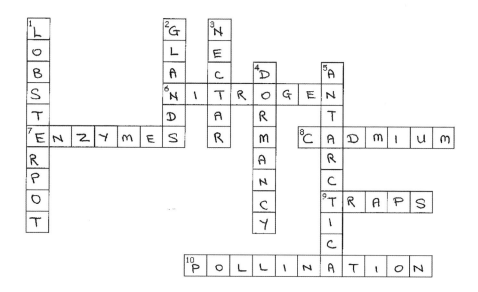

Across

6. An essential nutrient for all plants
7. These help carnivorous plants digest their prey
8. This metal is harmful to carnivorous plants
9. Carnivorous plants use these to catch their prey
10. Carnivorous plants attract insects for ? and nutrition.

Down

1. This is a passive trap
2. Secrete sticky substances
3. Sweet sugary secretions produced by plants
4. A period of rest for carnivorous plants that is similar to hibernation for certain animals
5. Carnivorous plants grow on every continent except this one

PREDATOR PLANTS WORD SEARCH

```
D  Y  F  F  A  T  S  I  C  D  Q  H  F  F  S
E  K  H  Q  Z  O  X  U  U  K  N  O  L  B  R
C  I  Q  M  W  G  L  I  X  U  Q  K  N  O  E
A  Z  I  E  O  I  E  G  T  C  Z  O  O  T  H
Y  A  K  O  T  Z  A  R  E  R  I  S  Z  A  C
T  H  Q  S  H  R  I  S  M  T  A  Y  N  N  T
N  C  M  C  M  T  E  N  A  I  K  P  M  I  I
X  E  N  V  I  R  O  N  M  E  N  T  S  S  P
M  K  F  O  Q  E  I  Q  E  J  Y  A  M  T  J
T  A  N  Z  V  L  D  W  V  I  A  R  T  S  C
R  O  O  I  L  Y  C  N  A  M  R  O  D  E  E
L  Q  R  O  P  S  D  O  I  N  J  H  D  J  S
F  H  P  R  X  E  S  X  Z  V  H  U  T  N  P
T  V  E  R  U  S  U  N  D  E  W  V  G  M  S
R  Y  L  C  I  Q  I  G  P  S  Q  A  M  Y  T
```

BOTANISTS	GERMINATES	PREY
DECAY	NUTRITION	SUNDEW
DORMANCY	PITCHERS	THRIVE
ENVIRONMENT	POLLINATION	TRAPS

WORDS IN A WORD

This is a list 25 words that can be obtained from the word 'carnivorous'. It is not an exhaustive list.

RACOONS	RUINS
AIRS	SARI
ARCS	SAVOR
ARSON	SCAN
COINS	SCAR
CORN	SCORN
CORONA	SCOUR
COUSIN	SONIC
CROONS	SOON
CURIO	SOUR
CURSOR	URNS
ICON	VAIN
INCUR	VANS
NOVA	VICAR
RAINS	VISON

PREDATOR PLANTS STRIKE AGAIN
DOUBLE PUZZLE SOLUTION

UNSCRAMBLED WORDS

EOPADRTR = PREDATOR

PYER = PREY

SANVORCIRUO = CANIVOROUS

TNSESIC = INSECTS

TTRSEINUN = NUTRIENTS

SRHECPIT = PITCHERS

NESDUSW = SUNDEWS

NASLDG = GLANDS

TAKE OUT ALL THE UNDERLINED LETTERS IN RED

T Y A V N R S P E U L

UNSCAMBLE THESE LETTERS & YOU WILL GET

VENUS FLYTRAP

PREDATOR PLANTS CROSSWORD 2

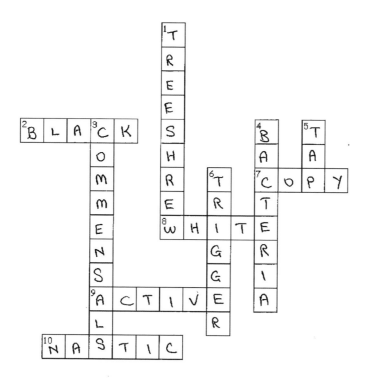

Across
2. Traps last a month or two before turning this color and falling off.
7. The best way to grow a Venus flytrap is to _____ their native habitat as much as possible.
8. Color of the flowers of the Venus flytrap
9. Some carnivorous plants have passive traps and some have _____ traps.
10. These movements are responses to stimuli but do not involve the growth of the plant.

Down
1. A mammal that is attracted by nectar to huge Nepenthes rajah.
3. A group of animals that come into contact with carnivorous plants without any danger.
4. Some carnivorous plants rely on this to produce the appropriate enzymes to help with digestion.
5. This type of water is not suitable for carnivorous plants because it is too alkaline and may contain too many minerals.
6. These hairs can be found on the inside of each lobe of the Venus flytrap.

PREDATOR PLANTS

MATCHING TERMS & CONCEPTS

d.   **Pitcher Plants**

c.   **Pollinators**

h.   **Humidity**

g.   **Roridula**

i.   **Nepenthes**

j.   **Dormancy**

e.   **Glands**

f.   **Active**

a.   **Cadmium**

b.   **Trigger**

Made in the USA
Columbia, SC
06 December 2017